Basic Supplies

Stretched Canvas
Hinges
Paint
Paintbrushes
Cardstock
Paper
Ribbon
Embellishments
Adhesive

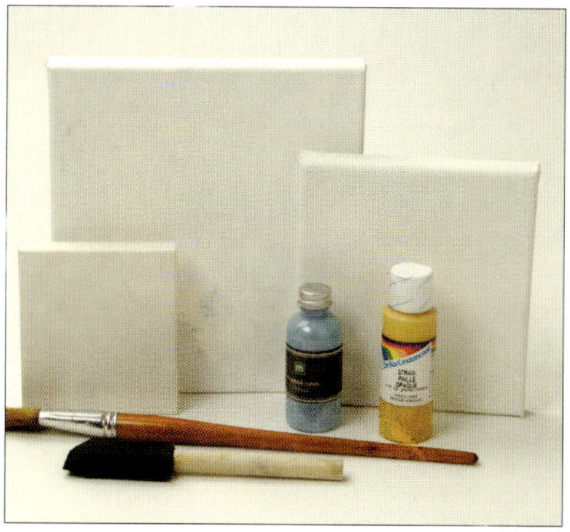

Index to Styles

Attach with Ties

Ribbon ties are a simple way to attach three or four canvas panels together. Ties are colorful, decorative and hold canvas triptychs firmly on any table.

1. Paint the canvas.

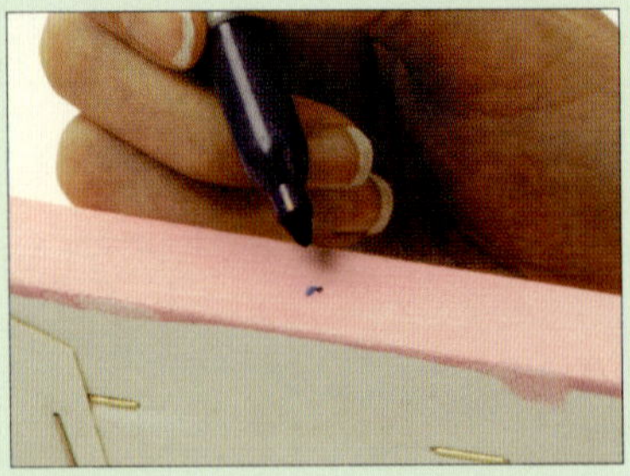

2. Mark canvases where the screw eyes will be attached.

3. Make small holes to 'start' the screw eyes.

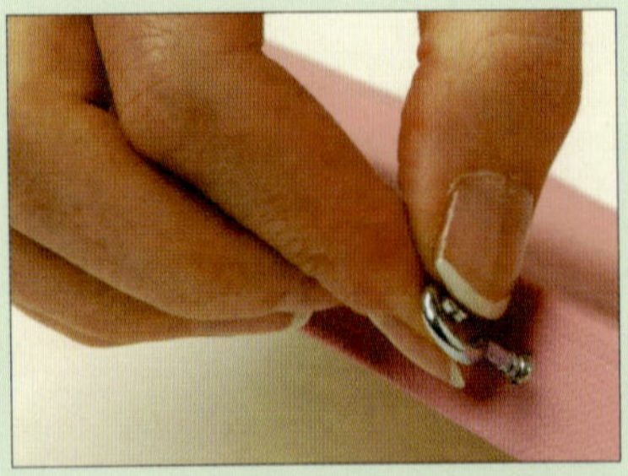

4. Attach screw eyes to canvases. Screw them in well.

5. Embellish the canvases as desired.

6. Tie the canvases together.

Joy

by Suzy West

Simply joyous! These canvases look great with their complementary colors, paper and design. Don't tell anyone how simple it is to create gorgeous art.

MATERIALS:
- Three 4" x 8" canvases
- Tan paint
- Van Dyke Brown ink pad
- 8 Screw eyes
- Decorative paper
- Twill
- Ribbon
- Metal Corners
- Rubber stamps
- Wood letters
- Silk daisy
- Photo Tape adhesive
- Glossy Accents adhesive

INSTRUCTIONS:
1. Paint wood letters. Let them dry. Ink the edges.
2. Adhere papers to the canvas.
3. Wrap twill all around each canvas.
4. Dry brush ink randomly around the canvas edges. Stamp words all around the canvases.
5. Adhere the metal corners with Glossy Accents.
6. Adhere photos in place.
7. Adhere the wood letters to each canvas spelling out joy.
8. Mark the ends of the canvases. Add screw eyes.
9. Decorate each screw eye with a ribbon.

Family Life

by Emelyn Magpoc

Family Life is very special. Celebrate it with this fun canvas layout. Large photos and small embellishments focus attention on the subject.

MATERIALS:
- Three 8" x 12" canvases
- Pink paint
- 8 Screw eyes
- Decorative paper
- Metal Signage
- Letter stickers
- Ribbons and/or fabric strips
- Flowers
- Pearl brads
- Photo Tape adhesive
- Glossy Accents adhesive

INSTRUCTIONS:
1. Paint canvases. Let dry.
2. Mark position of eye screws. Attach screw eyes.
3. Connect canvases with fabric strips.
4. Adhere photos to canvas.

Side canvases:

5. Adhere decorative papers to canvas.
6. Tie strips of ribbons to a strip of decorative paper. Adhere to canvas.
7. Adhere letter stickers.
8. Adhere Metal Signage to the right canvas.

Middle canvas:

9. Insert brads in the flower centers, through the decorative papers.
10. Adhere decorative paper with the flowers to the canvas.

To Be 4

by Emelyn Magpoc

Preserve the joys of being four years old with a trio of decorated canvases. Coordinate papers and embellishments with your photographs to capture a special moment, event, or day.

MATERIALS:
- Three 8" x 8" canvases
- Paint (Blue, Green)
- Brown Chalk ink
- 8 eye screws
- Decorative paper - *SEI*
- Stickers
- Ribbons
- Fabric pocket
- Wood number, Turtle
- Grass, Paper clip
- Photo Tape adhesive
- Glossy Accents adhesive

INSTRUCTIONS:
1. Paint canvases. Let dry.
2. Ink edges of canvases.
3. Mark and attach eye screws.
4. Connect canvases with ribbon.

Side canvases:

5. Adhere pictures to photo mat.
6. Ink edges of photo mat, decorative papers, and stickers.
7. Adhere decorative paper and matted photo.
8. Adhere stickers.

Middle canvas:

9. Paint wood number. Let dry.
10. Ink edges of number, decorative paper, and letter stickers.
11. Adhere decorative paper and photo to canvas.
12. Adhere turtle and grass in place.
13. Adhere fabric pocket over turtle and grass. Attach paper clip to pocket.
14. Adhere letter stickers and wooden number to canvas.

Holiday Memories

by Michelle Tornay

Holidays give us so many treasured moments. Celebrate the memories with a trio of canvases that are as easy to make as stuffing the stockings or plugging in the Christmas tree lights.

MATERIALS:
- Three 8" x 8" canvases
- Sage Green paint
- Van Dyke Brown ink
- 8 eye screws
- Wood frame
- Cranberry paper
- Letter stickers
- Ribbon
- 4 poinsettias
- Staple gun
- Photo Tape adhesive

INSTRUCTIONS:
1. Paint the canvases and frame. Let dry.
2. Ink all canvas and frame edges.
3. Mark and attach eye screws.
4. Cut one paper 4" x 8". Adhere to the bottom half of the center canvas.
5. Cut 8 paper squares 3¾" x 3¾". Ink all edges. Adhere 4 squares to each side canvas.
6. Insert photo into wooden frame.
7. Staple wooden frame to the middle canvas.
8. Adhere "Holiday Memories" letter stickers in place.
9. Adhere pictures and flowers as in photo.
10. Tie the canvases together.

Family is Everything

by Michelle Tornay

Canvas allows you to use layering and embellishment techniques. You'll enjoy scrapbooking on canvas to create exciting layouts.

MATERIALS:
- Three 6" x 6" canvases
- Blue paint
- Van Dyke Brown ink
- 12 eye screws
- Decorative paper
- Canvas flowers
- Rub-On words
- Blue fabric
- Pliers
- Photo Tape adhesive
- Glossy Accents adhesive

INSTRUCTIONS:
1. Paint the edges of all 3 canvases. Let dry.
2. Screw 3 eye screws into both sides of the center canvas and into 1 side of the other two canvases.
3. Hook the open end of the eye screw into the closed end and close the eye screws with pliers.
4. Tie fabric strips around the eye screws.
5. Cut three 6" paper squares. Ink the edges and adhere to the canvases.
6. Cut 6 papers 2" x 6". Ink the edges. Sew a Zigzag stitch across each strip. Adhere to the canvases.
7. Adhere photos in place.
8. Apply Rub-On words and adhere canvas flowers.

MATERIALS:
- Four 4" x 8" canvases
- Pastel Blue color wash - *7gypsies*
- 12 eye screws
- Decorative paper
- Alphabet stickers
- Metal tags
- Ribbon
- Circle punch
- Dirty Ego font
- Photo Tape adhesive
- Glossy Accents adhesive

INSTRUCTIONS:
1. Dry brush all edges of canvases.
2. Attach canvases together using screw eyes.
3. Embellish the canvases as desired.
4. Tie ribbons around the screw eyes.

Siblings

by Krista Fernandez

Eye hooks connect these canvases to make a screen. A great way to decorate your child's room with the faces of friends and relatives, this technique allows you to choose the size and number of canvases that suits your subject.

Grandma would love a set of canvases with all the grandchildren. Make one for a Mother's Day or birthday gift that will really be appreciated.

For Mom

by Michele Tornay

Nothing says "I love you, Mom" like flowers from the hand of your child. Dried flowers will fade but the memory won't if you capture the moment on film and preserve it on this canvas layout.

MATERIALS:
- Two 8" x 8" canvases
- One 8" x 12" canvas
- Paint (White, Lavender)
- Van Dyke Brown ink
- 8 eye screws
- Decorative paper
- Chipboard letters
- Circle tag
- White flowers
- Ribbon
- Metal buttons
- Letter stickers
- Photo Tape adhesive

INSTRUCTIONS:
1. Paint chipboard letters White. Let dry.
2. Paint the canvas edges Lavender. Let dry.
3. Ink the edges of the chipboard letters.
4. Cut 2 squares of decorative paper 8" x 8". Ink the edges. Adhere to 8" canvases.
5. Adhere an 8" x 12" photo to the large canvas.
6. Cut 5 strips of paper for title canvas. Ink the edges. Glue in place. Adhere chipboard letters in place. Cover circle tag with paper. Add stickers, flower, button, and ribbon. Glue tag in place.
7. Cut a 6" x 8" mat for the bottom canvas. Ink the edges. Adhere mat and photo to canvas.
8. Cut paper 1" x 8". Ink the edges. Adhere flowers and button to strip. Adhere strip as in photo.
9. Screw eye screws into the canvases as shown in photo.
10. Tie all of the canvases together.

Family

by Krista Fernandez

Create a sense of water with colorwash paint and light blue papers. You can almost smell the salt in the surf as you look at these great photos.

MATERIALS:
- Three 8" x 8" canvases
- Colorwash - *7gypsies*
- Van Dyke Brown ink
- 8 screw eyes
- Decorative paper
- Chipboard letters
- Twine
- Flowers
- Ribbon
- Photo Tape adhesive

INSTRUCTIONS:
1. Colorwash all canvases. Let dry.
2. Coat chipboard letters with colorwash. Let dry and then ink edges with Brown. Set aside.
3. Embellish canvases with photos, chipboard letters, twine and flowers.
4. Attach screw eyes. Tie canvases together.

MATERIALS:
- Three 8" x 8" canvases
- Beige paint
- Van Dyke Brown ink
- 8 eye screws
- Wood frame
- Decorative paper
- Letter stickers
- Ribbon
- 4 Blue flowers
- Staple gun
- Photo Tape adhesive

INSTRUCTIONS:
1. Paint the canvases and frame. Let dry.
2. Ink all canvas and frame edges.
3. Screw eye screws into the canvases as shown in the photo.
4. Cut one paper 4" x 8". Adhere to the bottom half of the center canvas.
5. Cut 8 paper squares 3¾" x 3¾". Ink all edges. Adhere 4 squares to each side canvas.
6. Insert photo into wooden frame.
7. Staple wooden frame to the middle canvas.
8. Adhere "Memories" letter stickers in place.
9. Adhere pictures and flowers as in photo.
10. Tie the canvases together.

Memories

by Suzy West

You can get an entirely different look just by changing the papers and colors on your canvas. Memories uses the same layout as Holiday Memories on page 7, yet they have an entirely different texture and tone.

Joy of Living

by Krista Fernandez

Let them be little, thrive on the joy, cherish the childlike wonder, and make sure you photograph precious moments.

Preserve the memories with delightful layouts like this one.

Attach with Hinges

Hinges make a secure attachment for three, four or more canvas panels. Use a screwdriver to secure hinges with small screws. The pieces can sit on a table or hang on the wall.

1. Paint the canvas panels.

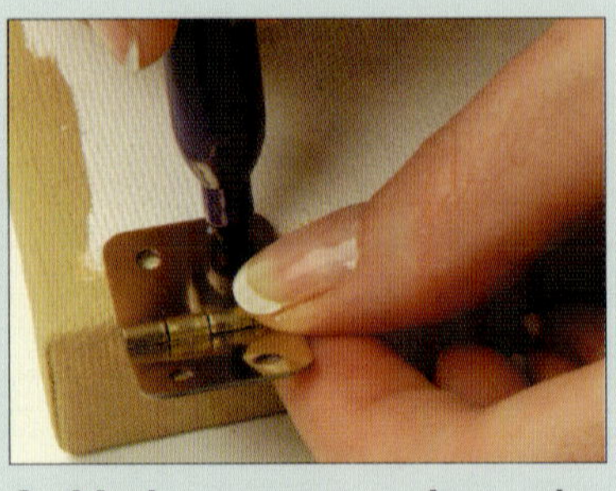

2. Mark canvases where the hinges will be attached.

3. Make small holes to 'start' the screws for the hinges

4. Attach hinges with small screws.

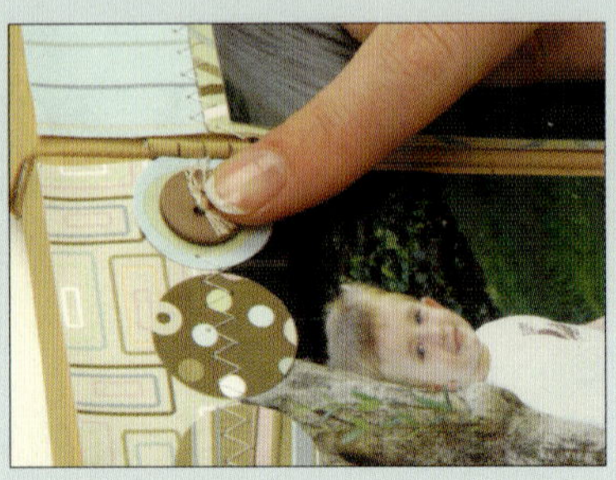

5. Embellish the canvases as desired.

Joy of Living

MATERIALS:

- One 8" x 8" canvas
- Two 4" x 8" canvases
- Shopping Bag acrylic paint
- 4 hinges
- Decorative paper
- Buttons, Metal letter, Brads
- "j", "o", "y" letters
- Embroidery thread
- Transparency film
- Circle punch
- Constitution font
- Sewing machine
- Photo Tape adhesive
- Adhesive Glossy Accents

INSTRUCTIONS:

1. Hinge the 3 canvases together.
2. Paint all canvas edges. Let dry.
3. Embellish the canvases.

Our Spot

MATERIALS:

- Two 4" x 8" canvases
- One 8" x 8" canvas
- Blue paint
- 4 hinges
- Small chipboard letters
- Circle tags
- Fabric strips
- Chipboard letters & heart
- Closure
- Photo Tape adhesive
- Glossy Accents adhesive

INSTRUCTIONS:

1. Paint the canvases. Let dry.
2. Arrange canvases as in photo. Mark holes and hinge canvases together.
3. Cut one 6" x 8" photo in half and adhere the two halves to the 4" x 8" canvases.
4. Adhere the chipboard letters to the top of the front 4" x 8" canvases to make the title.
5. Adhere the closures to the top and bottom canvases
6. Embellish the inside of the canvases with photos, circle tags, letters, chipboard heart and fabric.

Our Spot

by Michelle Tornay

Marshall proposed right underneath the Golden Gate bridge and nearly dropped the ring in the water. We took Angel and Daniel to the bridge for our first family outing. It's our favorite family destination. It's Our Spot!

Remember this easy project next time you take photos of your family's favorite place.

Love

by Suzy West

Wood letters are easy to find and allow you to create a title with solidity and dimension. Use this set of canvases as a table screen or dresser decoration.

MATERIALS:

- One 8" x 12" canvas
- Two 4" x 8" canvases
- Burgundy paint
- 4 hinges
- Decorative paper
- Rickrack
- Wood letters
- Photo Tape adhesive
- Glossy Accents adhesive

INSTRUCTIONS:

1. Paint all the canvases and the wood letters. Let dry.
2. Cut papers to size and adhere to the canvas.
3. Adhere rickrack, wood letters, and photo to the canvas.
4. Hinge the canvases together.

WHY I LOVE YA INSTRUCTIONS:

1. Paint canvases. Let dry.
2. Attach 4" canvases to 4" x 8" canvas with hinges.

Front of the canvas left side:

3. Ink edges of the decorative papers and sticker tab.
4. Adhere to photo.
5. Adhere photo to decorative paper.
6. Attach flowers with a brad in the center.
7. Adhere decorative paper/photo to the canvas.

Front of the canvas, right side:

8. Ink edges of the decorative papers.
9. Tie ribbon to a strip of decorative paper.
10. Adhere decorative papers to the canvas.
11. Apply letter stickers and rub-ons for the title.

Left and Right Inside canvas:

12. Ink edges of decorative papers and adhere to canvas.
13. Adhere photo to the left canvas.
14. Adhere tab to photo on right canvas. Adhere photo.

Middle canvas:

15. Fold an 8" square of decorative paper in half.
16. Adhere photo to the front of the fold.
17. Adhere inked sticker next to the photo.
18. Tie ribbons on a strip of paper, adhere below sticker.
19. Attach brad to flower and glue next to the sticker.
20. Attach flowers with brads to inside of folded paper.
21. Adhere photo on 3 edges, creating a pocket.
22. Adhere tab to inked tags. Adhere letter stickers.
23. Write reasons on the tags and insert in the pocket.
24. Attach photo anchors with brads, use as a closure.

MATERIALS:
- One 4" x 8" canvas
- Two 4" x 4" canvases
- Tan paint
- Tan Chalk ink
- 2 hinges
- Decorative paper
- Letter stickers, Rub-On
- Stickers and tabs, Ribbons
- Brads, Photo anchors
- Flowers
- Photo Tape adhesive
- Glossy Accents adhesive

Why I Love Ya

by Emelyn Magpoc

He says...She says...

The most romantic aspect of this canvas is the journaling on the tags. She wrote one to him, and he wrote one to her.

So often we do not take time to tell those we love how much we appreciate them. This is the perfect opportunity to tell your spouse what you love about him or her.

This romantic canvas set with its special journaling will be a keepsake to pass down to future generations.

Turn the photo tabs and another flap comes down revealing yet another photo. Journaling tags live in the pocket formed by the flap.

Sweet Dewey

by Michelle Tornay

Dewey is the sweetest dog a family could ever have. He is everyone's favorite. When you make your canvas layouts, don't forget the furry members of the family.

MATERIALS:

- Two 4" x 8" canvases
- One 8" x 12" canvas
- Blue paint
- Van Dyke Brown ink
- 4 hinges
- Decorative paper
- Fabric strips
- Wooden tags
- Rub-On letters
- Photo Tape adhesive
- Glossy Accents adhesive

INSTRUCTIONS:

1. Paint the canvases. Let dry.
2. Rub letters onto the wooden tags.
3 Tie fabric through the holes on the wooden tags
4. Cut Polka Dot paper 8" x 12" Cut Floral paper 8" x 11".
5. Zigzag stitch the Floral paper to the Polka dot paper and adhere to the large canvas.
6. Cut 2 Polka Dot papers 4" x 8". Cut 2 Floral papers 4" x 6". Adhere Floral paper to the middle of the Polka dot paper.
7. Zigzag stitch the Floral paper to the Polka dot paper and adhere to the small canvases.
8. Mark holes for hinges on the inside of the 4" x 8" canvases and on both sides of the 8" x 12" canvas.
9. Hinge canvases together.
10. Adhere the wooden tags and photo in place.

MATERIALS:
- One 4" x 8" canvas
- Two 4" x 4" canvases
- Apple Barrel Rose Bouquet acrylic paint
- Ink (Van Dyke Brown, Lamp Black)
- 2 hinges
- Decorative paper
- Ribbon
- Silk flower
- Williamsburg lower case alphabet stamps - *Technique Tuesday*
- Carbonated Gothic font
- Sewing machine, Staples
- Photo Tape adhesive
- Glossy Accents adhesive

INSTRUCTIONS:
1. Paint all canvases. Let dry.
2. Hinge the 3 canvases together.
3. Embellish the cover and insides as desired.

CKU

by Krista Fernandez

Creating Keepsakes University is pure scrapbooking passion. Attending these classes creates memories as well as layouts. The tags list celebrities I met and the classes I attended. The photos record the experiences shared with wonderful friends.

When one canvas cannot possibly contain all the fun, hinging two small canvases to a larger one provides that much needed extra surface.

Waterfalls & Fold-Outs

Attach several canvases together with hinges to create these surprise fold-out displays. Folds can be vertical, horizontal and multiple.

1. Paint the canvas.

2. Mark canvases where the hinges will be attached.

3. Make small holes to 'start' the screws for the hinges

4. Attach hinges to one edge with small screws.

5. Attach hinges to the paired edge. Be sure they are even.

6. Embellish the canvases as desired.

MATERIALS:
- Two 4" x 4" canvas
- One 8" x 12" canvas
- One 8" x 8" canvases
- Brick Red paint
- Van Dyke Brown ink
- 4 hinges
- Decorative paper - *Chatterbox*
- Transparency
- Chipboard letters, Deco brads
- Flowers
- English 111 Vouace BT font
- Photo Tape adhesive
- Glossy Accents adhesive

INSTRUCTIONS:
1. Paint the canvases. Let dry.
2. Place the two 4" canvases on top of the 8" x 12" canvas and mark the holes for the hinges.
3. Place the 8" canvas on top of the 8" x 12" canvas and mark the holes for the hinges.
4. Hinge the canvases together so that the 4" canvases swing open to the left and the 8" canvas swings open to the right.
5. Adhere photos to the 4" canvases.
6. Cut an 8" square of decorative paper and 2 strips of coordinated paper ½" x 8".
7. Adhere the strips to the bottom and top of the 8" paper and sew a Zigzag stitch.
8. Print out the words "Celebrate Life's" on a transparency.
9. Trim the transparency to 8" x 8" and adhere in place with Glossy Accents.
10. Ink the chipboard letters.
11. Adhere the deco brads to the center of each flower.
12. Adhere the letters and flowers to the canvas.
13. Adhere photos in place.

Special Moments

by Michelle Tornay

Cesare Pavese said, "We do not remember days, we remember moments. The richness of life lies in the memories we have forgotten." Appreciate the richness of life with a tribute to those special moments. This set of canvases will preserve those special times for years to come.

Our Beautiful Son

by Michelle Tornay

Next time you take photos of the kids at the skateboard park or playing their favorite sport, remember this great layout and take many pictures.

MATERIALS:
- Two 4" x 4" canvases
- One 4" x 8" canvas
- Green paint
- Van Dyke Brown ink
- 4 hinges
- Cardstock
- Decorative paper
- Chipboard letters
- Brads
- Furniture tacks
- Wooden tag
- Word stickers
- Ribbon
- Photo Tape adhesive
- Glossy Accents adhesive

All six of these photos were shot at the same time for a more complete story about a day or an event in your child's life.

INSTRUCTIONS:
1. Paint the edges of all canvases and the brads. Let dry.
2. Join the small canvases to the large canvas with hinges.

Front cover:

3. Cut a paper strip 1½" x 4". Sew a Zigzag stitch across the strip. Adhere paper strip, wooden tag and chipboard letters in place. Adhere a sticker to the wooden tag.
4. Crop three 4" square photos. Adhere to the top and bottom canvases.
5. Cut cardstock 8" x 12". Score every 4" along the 12" side. Accordion fold.
6. Cut 2 paper strips ½" x 12". Sew a Zigzag stitch along the center of the strip.
7. Adhere three 4" x 6" photos in place. Adhere paper strips, word stickers and brads.
8. Adhere accordion to the large canvas.
9. Push furniture tacks into the inside of each opening side of the canvases
10. Tie ribbons around the furniture tacks to hold the book closed.

MATERIALS:
- One 8" x 12" canvas
- Two 4" x 4" canvases
- Two 4" x 8" canvases
- Yellow paint
- Van Dyke Brown ink
- 8 hinges
- Decorative paper - *Chatterbox*
- Chipboard letters
- Ribbon
- Flowers
- Photo Tape adhesive
- Glossy Accents adhesive

INSTRUCTIONS:

1. Paint all the canvases and the chipboard letters. Let dry.
2. Adhere papers to the canvases.
3. Adhere ribbons, flowers, and chipboard letters to the canvas.
4. Adhere center photo.
5. Hinge canvases together.

True Love

by Suzy West

The colors in this canvas fold-out come right out of the photo, creating a unified piece of art instead of the usual photo hanging in a frame.

Although this layout would work well in any scrapbook, it is much more fun to have this dimensional collection of canvases on your desk, coffee table, or dresser where you can share it with family and enjoy it every day.

Flower Girl

by Emelyn Magpoc

A layout is so much more than a photo. A good layout provides context to the viewer. Ribbon embellishments and a title turn this photo into a great canvas layout.

MATERIALS:
- One 8" x 12" canvas
- Four 4" x 4" canvases
- Yellow Green paint
- Brown Chalk ink
- 4 hinges
- Decorative paper - *SEI*
- Monogram coasters - *SEI*
- Letter stickers, Rub-On, Tag
- Flowers
- Rhinestone brad, Ribbons
- Photo anchors
- Photo Tape adhesive
- Glossy Accents adhesive

INSTRUCTIONS:
1. Paint canvases. Let dry.
2. Ink edges of canvases.
3. Attach 4" canvases to 8" x 12" canvas with hinges.
4. Adhere photo to canvas.
5. Ink edges of decorative paper and monogram coasters.
6. Adhere decorative paper in place.
7. Punch a hole in the "I" monogram. Add a ribbon.
8. Adhere monogram coasters to decorative paper.
9. Tie ribbons on photo anchors and adhere to canvas, connecting decorative paper and photo.
10. Adhere letter stickers. Apply rub-on word to photo.
11. Tie ribbon on tag and adhere to photo.
12. Insert a rhinestone brad in the center of the flower.

Hawaii

by Krista Fernandez

Paradise is defined as a place of complete bliss. When your vacation is truly "Paradise Found", hold the bliss in the forefront of your mind. Even on your most stressful work day, this set of canvases will take you back to those fun-filled sunny days every time you look at them and help you remember that "Life is Good!"

This is definitely a canvas set to keep in your office cubicle or on top of your monitor.

Be sure to check out the technique for making this beautiful watercolor title on the front of this canvas.

MATERIALS:
- One 8" x 12" canvas
- One 8" x 8" canvas
- Two 4" x 4" canvases
- Sparkle finish
- Pastel Blue color wash - *7gypsies*
- Daiquiri paint
- 4 hinges
- Decorative paper - *Scenic Route*
- Ribbon, Silk flowers
- Label maker
- Photo anchors, Brads
- Foam alphabet stamps
- Circle punch, Staples
- Heber Font - *Chatterbox*
- Brownie font - *Creating Keepsakes*
- Photo Tape adhesive
- Glossy Accents adhesive

INSTRUCTIONS:
1. Paint the canvases with color wash. Let dry.
2. Hinge all 4 canvases together.
3. Adhere photo to the 8" x 8" canvas.
4. Stamp the title. Let dry.
5. Coat with Delta Sparkle finish.
6. Embellish the other canvases as desired.

Only Me

by Suzy West

Who am I? Mom, daughter, friend, sister, wife, aunt. Handwritten journaling makes this canvas art very personal.

I wish my grandmother had made something like this so my children could know more about who she was.

MATERIALS:
- One 4" x 8" canvas
- Two 4" x 4" canvases
- Red paint
- 4 hinges
- Cardstock
- Decorative paper
- Stickers
- Ribbon
- Metal embellishments
- Stencils
- Rub-Ons
- Photo Tape adhesive
- Glossy Accents adhesive

INSTRUCTIONS:

1. Paint canvases. Let dry.
2. **Inside**: Cover the large canvas with paper. Adhere photo and ribbon in place.
3. Cut 2 Red cardstock strips 4" x 11½". Fold into a 3 part accordion.
4. **Inside Top canvas**: Arrange the accordion so it opens coming down. Add photo and titles with stickers, metal words and rub-ons as shown in photo. Adhere accordion to the inside of the canvas.
5. **Outside Top canvas**: Adhere a photo and a metal corner in place.
6. **Inside Bottom canvas**: Arrange the accordion so it opens to the right. Record journaling. Adhere photo.
7. **Outside Bottom canvas**: Cover canvas with decorative paper. Add stencils, rub-on, metal flower and metal corners.
8. Hinge the canvases together.

Grandpa & Company

by Michelle Tornay

Grandparents are a family's greatest treasure, the founders of a loving legacy, the greatest storytellers, and the keepers of traditions that linger on in cherished memory. Celebrate the legacy with this collection of canvases.

MATERIALS:
- One 4" x 8" canvas
- One 8" x 12" canvas
- Four 4" x 4" canvases
- Brown paint
- Van Dyke Brown ink
- 5 hinges
- Decorative paper - *SEI*
- Coasters, Letter stickers, Rub-Ons
- Ribbon, Silk daisies
- Transparency
- Furniture tacks
- Photo Tape adhesive
- Glossy Accents adhesive

INSTRUCTIONS:
1. Paint the canvases. Let dry.
2. Arrange canvases as in photo. Mark holes and hinge canvases together.
3. Cut out two 4" squares of Argyle paper. Cut one 4" x 8" rectangle of Aqua.
4. Sew a Running stitch around all of the decorative paper.
5. Adhere ribbon across bottom of 2 papers. Rub words in place. Adhere daisy.
6. Adhere the coaster and stickers to the 4" x 8" paper to form the title.
7. Adhere the decorative papers and photos to the appropriate canvases.
8. Print journaling on a transparency to fit on the 4" x 8" canvas. Adhere over paper with Glossy Accents.
9. Push the furniture tacks in place and tie the canvases together with a ribbon.

Only an Aunt

by Suzy West

Only an aunt can give hugs like a mother, can keep secrets like a sister, and share love like a friend. Celebrate special relationships with a set of coordinated art canvases.

This delightful hinged grouping opens to reveal a beautiful collection of photos.

MATERIALS:

- Three 4" x 8" canvases
- One 8" x 12" canvases
- Sage paint
- 6 hinges
- Decorative paper
- White daisy trim
- Silk daisy
- Transparency
- Photo Tape adhesive
- Glossy Accents adhesive

INSTRUCTIONS:

1. Paint all the canvases. Let them dry.
2. **Title Canvas:** Adhere decorative paper. Print title on transparency and adhere it to the canvas with Glossy Accents.
3. Turn the title canvas over, keeping in mind where the hinges will be so your photo will be right side up. Adhere photo, paper and daisy trim to the canvas.
5. **Bottom Canvases**: Adhere photos to both sides of the bottom 4" x 8" canvases. Add strips of decorative paper and daisy trim.
6. **Center Canvas**: Adhere an 8" x 12" photo to the large center canvas.
7. **Finish**: Connect canvases with hinges. Adhere daisy trim and silk daisy to the title canvas.

All American

by Emelyn Magpoc

Show off your patriotic spirit and support for our military with a canvas collection that shouts Proud to be American!

MATERIALS:
- One 8" x 12" canvas
- 12" x 12" canvas
- Three 4" x 4" canvases
- Tan paint
- Van Dyke Brown ink
- 5 hinges
- Decorative paper - *K&Company*
- Stickers, Metal charms
- Brads
- Transparency
- Netting
- Toys - *Matchbox*
- Armymen Font - *Chatterbox*
- Staple gun
- Glossy Accents adhesive

INSTRUCTIONS:

1. Paint all canvases. Let dry.

Assemble canvases:

2. Attach 8" x 12" canvas to 12" x 12" canvas with 2 hinges.
3. Attach each small canvas to the bottom with a hinge.

Front cover:

4. Staple decorative paper to the 8" x 12" canvas back.
5. Staple netting over the decorative paper.
6. Adhere military toys.
7. Print "USA" on transparency to fit on 4" squares.
8. Cut 4" squares of decorative paper. Ink the edges.
9. Cover with transparency. Staple to canvases.

Inside:

10. Print "All American" on transparency. Ink the edges of an 8" x 12" decorative paper. Cover with transparency and staple to canvas.
11. Staple decorative paper to the large canvas and adhere photo.
12. Staple decorative paper to each small canvas and adhere photos.
13. Adhere metal charms and stickers.

Pull the hinged panels up at the top and down at the bottom to reveal all the photos.

Accordion Fold-Outs

The fun pages in these books fold out to display photos and memorabilia. Show off your treasured memories in a story book format.

1. Paint the canvas.

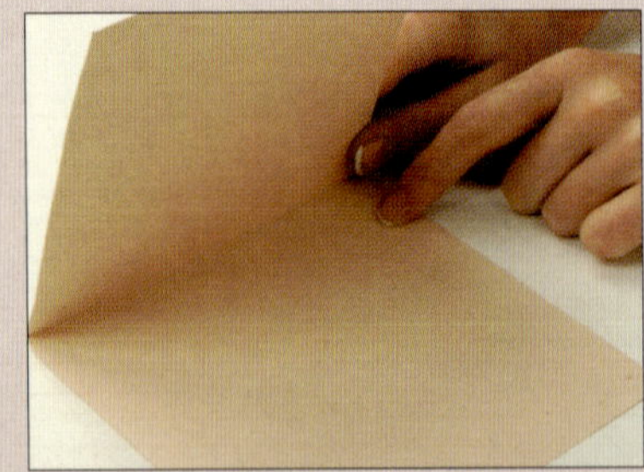

2. Cut cardstock and fold.

3. Attach papers end to end to make a longer strip.

4. Adhere accordion book to the inside of the canvases.

5. Sandwich the ribbon between canvas and cover.

6. Embellish as desired.

Now and Forever

by Krista Fernandez

Break away from the usual wedding photo album with a picture perfect accordion book. Share the excitement of pre-ceremony preparations with beautifully matted photos that are presented with rub-on titles. Little white flower embellishments and ribbons complete the layout with simple elegance.

Take this idea and apply it to other special occasions such as bridal and baby showers or parties celebrating birthdays, retirement, and graduation.

This book is quick to assemble, but looking at the results will take you back to that special memory Now and Forever.

MATERIALS:
- Two 6" x 6" canvases
- Touch O Pink acrylic paint
- Decorative paper - *Chatterbox*
- Rub-On letters
- Stickers
- Heart brads
- Photo corners
- Flowers, Ribbon
- Staples, Sewing machine
- Photo Tape adhesive
- Glossy Accents adhesive

INSTRUCTIONS:
1. Paint canvases. Let dry.
2. Cut 3 strips of cardstock 5⅞" x 11¾". Fold in half.
3. Adhere a piece of coordinating decorative paper to the seams of each strip of cardstock.
4. Zigzag stitch the seams together using a sewing machine.
5. Adhere accordion book to the insides on the canvases.
6. Adhere ribbon across the middle of the front cover.
7. Embellish the accordion book and cover of the canvas using photos, decorative paper, ribbon, photo corners and rub-on words and stickers.

Girl Time

by Krista Fernandez

A day out shopping or a night out with girlfriends always creates treasured moments full of laughter and stories.

This accordion book has plenty of pages for our photos, our stories, and our secrets so we never forget all the good times we shared and how silly we were.

INSTRUCTIONS:

1. Paint canvases. Let dry.
2. Create an accordion album using Black cardstock.
3. Embellish album and adhere it to the backs of the 2 canvases.
4 Staple ribbon to the front and back of the book to tie the book closed.
5. Embellish the front cover with tags and flowers.

MATERIALS:

- Two 4" x 4" canvases
- Boysenberry Pink acrylic paint
- Black cardstock
- Decorative paper - *7gypsies, KI Memories*
- Rub-Ons
- Tags
- Ribbon
- Rhinestones
- Glass marble
- Flower punch, Stapler
- Fonts (Stenography, Rubber stamp, Top Secret) - *Creating Keepsakes*
- Photo Tape adhesive
- Glossy Accents adhesive

Kauai

by Michelle Tornay

Looking for a unique closure? D-rings and ribbons keep this accordion album fastened. Inside, the journaling is printed on clear transparency and mounted over a light printed paper.

MATERIALS:
- Two 4" x 4" canvases
- Light Blue paint
- Van Dyke Brown ink
- 2 D-rings
- Cardstock
- Decorative paper - *Scrapworks*
- Chipboard letter
- Ribbon
- Rub-Ons
- Paper sayings
- Rubber stamps - *Technique Tuesday*
- Silk daisy
- Wooden flower
- Tags
- Avant Garde BK BT font
- Photo Tape adhesive
- Glossy Accents adhesive

INSTRUCTIONS:
1. Paint canvases. Let dry.
2. Stamp sayings around the outside of the canvases.
3. Nail the D-rings to the side of one of the canvases.
4. Cut 3 strips of paper that measure 4" x 12".
5. Score the paper every 4 inches. Each strip should be stored 3 times.
6. Attach the papers end-to-end to make an 8-page accordion.
7. Adhere each end of the accordion to the two canvases.
8. Cut a 4" square of paper. Ink the edges. Adhere to the canvas.
9. Cut a 3¾" square of paper for the title. Sew a Zigzag stitch around it. Ink the edges. Adhere in place.
10. Paint the letter. Let dry.
11. Tie a ribbon around the letter and adhere in place.
12. Rub on the letters to finish the title.
13. Adhere silk and wood flowers in place.
14. Tie ribbons around the D-rings to hold the album closed.

Inside:

Page 1: Adhere light decorative paper and ribbons. Print journaling on a transparency and adhere with Glossy Accents.

Pages 2, 4, 6, 8: Adhere photo.

Page 3: Punch a hole in the side of the photo. Insert ribbons and tie bows. Adhere to page.

Page 4: Adhere papers and photo.

Page 5: Stamp the page with a large background stamp. Cut a 4" square of paper or cardstock. Cut the upper right corner off. Punch holes along the cut edge. Insert ribbons and tie bows. Adhere to page to form a pocket. Adhere a silk daisy. Decorate a tag with a small photo and journaling. Add a ribbon to the tag and tuck it into the pocket.

Page 7: Adhere a photo to a 3½" x 4" cardstock. Adhere this to the page to make a pocket. Tuck a journaling tag into the pocket.

'H' - Happy

by Suzy West

Holiday Memories are some of the most special, for 'tis the season to gather family and friends who often live miles apart.

This accordion book holds photos as well as memorabilia. Use journal tags to record your favorite traditions. Ribbons and holiday papers make simple pockets to hold journal tags, while favorite photos bedeck the facing pages.

Create a unique closure for this book by adhering a piece of velcro to the back of the Christmas doll.

MATERIALS:
- Two 4" x 4" canvases
- Beige & Green paint
- Van Dyke Brown ink
- Greenbriar cardstock
- Decorative paper - *Provo Craft, Autumn Leaves, Scenic Route*
- Wood letter
- Ribbons, Tags
- Metal embellishments
- Epoxy stickers
- Label maker
- Doll Christmas ornament
- Fabric strips, Index tab
- Flowers, Staple Gun
- Velcro
- Photo Tape adhesive
- Glossy Accents adhesive

INSTRUCTIONS:

1. Paint canvases Beige and wood letter Green. Let dry.
2. Cut 3 strips of cardstock 4" x 12". Score each strip every 4". Fold and adhere ends of accordion together.

First page:

3. Cover with decorative paper. Computer print a calendar page, staple in place. Add flower, labels, ribbons and embellishments.

Pages 2, 4, 6:

4. Adhere photo in place.

Third page:

5. Adhere decorative paper to page. Cut a 2" x 4" strip of paper and adhere 3 edges to the base page creating a pocket. Adhere ribbon in place. Design small tags and staple ribbons to the top. Place tags the pocket. Add index tab to the top of the page.

Fifth page:

6. Repeat steps for third page. Staple strips to edges of page. Journal on a large tag, add strips. Highlight words with epoxy stickers. Add embellishments.

Assembly:

7. Adhere the accordion to your canvases. Make sure you have plenty of adhesives. Staple a little doll to the left edge of canvas.
8. On the back of her right side, add a strip of Velcro. Place the opposite side of Velcro on the edge of right side of canvas as a closure.

Book Covers:

Cover canvas with decorative paper. Add a strip of paper on the bottom, decorate with ribbon. Glue a wood letter to left side of canvas. Add music paper, label words and a flower on the right side.

Batman Book

by Emelyn Magpoc

Nice suit! And today you are? Batman!

This accordion book is all about play, pretend, imagination and fun. Who needs television and theatre when you can create your own hero in the backyard!

Capture the excitement with photos that tell the amazing story. And remember to call Alfred if you are going to be late for dinner.

MATERIALS:
- Two 4" x 4" canvases
- Brown Chalk Ink
- Decorative paper - *Gin-X*
- Rub-On letters
- Stickers
- Canvas phrases
- Brads
- Photo anchors
- Fabric strips
- Photo Tape adhesive
- Glossy Accents adhesive

INSTRUCTIONS:
1. Ink all edges of canvases with ink.

Create accordion book:

2. Cut 2 strips of cardstock 4" x 12". Fold into thirds and ink edges.
3. Cut a 4" x 8" strip of cardstock and fold in half. Use this strip to attach the 2 longer strips.
4. Decorate pages as desired.

Assembly:

5. Adhere book to inside of canvas.
6. Cut a 24" strip of fabric. Wrap the fabric around both canvases so it will tie shut and adhere to canvas.
7. Cover the front and back of the canvas with decorative paper.
8. Embellish the front cover.

Shadow Boxes

Display photos and memories every day. Small canvas panels have a crevice where you can store and enjoy memorabilia.

You'll love these attractive canvas nichos with photos of loved ones, sentimental titles, embellishments and special events.

Simple canvases can be displayed on your favorite table or right on the wall.

1. Paint the canvas.

2. Embellish as desired.

3. Display open canvas on a table.

MATERIALS:

- Two 8" x 8" Chunky canvases
- Peach color wash - *7gypsies*
- Van Dyke Brown ink
- 2 hinges
- Decorative paper - *Wild Asparagus*
- Rub-On letters, Stickers
- Silk flower
- Photo corners
- Circle punch
- Glossy Accents adhesive

Ban del ier

by Krista Fernandez

The depth and dimension of the caverns at Bandelier were just begging to be presented in a 3-d shadowbox format. The canvas window provides a great way to display not only photographs, but the maps, tickets, and memories of a double duty adventure. Bandelier gave us both excitement and relaxation, exploration and solitude. We came back from this trip refreshed and inspired by an unforgettable experience.

INSTRUCTIONS:

1. Paint the canvases with color wash. Let dry.
2. Hinge canvases together, back to back.
3. Cover the front with large circles and a photo.
4. Use alphabet rub-ons to create the title.
5. Cover the frame of the backs of the canvases with decorative paper.
6. Fill the inside of the book with mementos and photos.

MATERIALS:
- Two 8" x 12" Canvases
- Paint (Yellow, Red, Black)
- 2 hinges
- Cardstock
- Decorative paper - *KI Memories*
- Ribbon
- Metal label holder
- Disney embellishments
- Letter stickers
- Rubber stamps (Dots, Letter) - *Technique Tuesday*
- Photo Tape adhesive
- Glossy Accents adhesive

INSTRUCTIONS:
1. Paint the canvases Yellow. Let them dry.
2. **Cover**: Cut White cardstock 4" x 7¾" for a title block. Stamp letters with Black paint. Let dry. Add embellishments for the title. Let dry. Adhere cardstock to the center of the canvas.
3. Cut 2 strips of Black cardstock 2" x 7¾". Adhere to canvas.
4. Add ribbons.
5. Stamp Red dots onto the Yellow part of the canvas.
6. **Inside**: Adhere paper, photos, and embellishments inside the window.
7. Cut Red cardstock frame to fit the outer part of the canvas.
8. Tie ribbons to the Red cardstock.
9. Cut and adhere ribbon to the canvas edges. Place cardstock over the canvas covering the ribbon.
10. Add stickers and other embellishments to the cardstock to decorate.
11. Close the book and screw the hinges on.

Magical Memories

by Suzy West

Keep the memories of that magical Disney vacation close at hand in this canvas memory book. It's a scrapbook and shadowbox all in one colorful creation. Display it open on a table top or like a book on a shelf.

MATERIALS:
- Two 8" x 8" Chunky canvases
- Brown paint
- Brown Chalk ink
- 2 hinges
- Decorative paper - *SEI*
- Letter stickers
- Sticker tabs
- Ribbon
- Keepsake pocket - *Pebbles, Inc.*
- Brads
- Fabric strip
- Watering can
- Metal sign
- Flowers
- Cup hook
- Popsicle stick
- Drill
- Glossy Accents adhesive

Bloom

by Emelyn Magpoc

These niches are filled with memories... each is a tribute to a growing gardener. My daughter loves flowers and often helps me water them. Seeing her with the watering can inspired the inside of this shadowbox.

I hope my daughter's love for gardening will continue to bloom as she grows, but even if it does not, this canvas box is a fond remembrance of the hours we shared together surrounded by the intoxicating scents and beauty of flowers.

INSTRUCTIONS:

1. Paint all sides of canvases. Let dry.
2. Hinge canvases together.

Inside both canvases:

3. Cut mitered strips of decorative paper to frame the "window".
4. Ink all edges and adhere to the canvas.
5. Cut decorative paper to fit inside the window. Ink edges and adhere in place.

Left side:

6. Drill 2 small holes in the inside of the watering can.
7. Attach cup hook to the corner of the window to hold the handle of the watering can. Tie fabric strip around the handle.
8. Attach watering can to the canvas with brads for added stability. Insert flowers in the watering can.
9. Apply inked letter stickers.

Right side:

10. Adhere photo inside the window.
11. Adhere metal sign to popsicle stick and adhere over the photo.
12. Adhere flowers and stickers.

Cover of the shadow box:

13. Trim decorative paper to fit cover. Ink the edges.
14. Layer inked decorative papers and adhere in place.
15. Adhere inked tab sticker to photo and adhere to canvas.
16. Use a brad to secure flower on the decorative paper.
17. Tie a ribbon on the keepsake pocket and adhere over the flower.

Princess Angel

by Michelle Tornay

What a unique disguise! This purse is actually a wonderful shadowbox book holding treasured memories of Sleeping Beauty's castle from our trip to Disneyland in 2004.

MATERIALS:

- One 8" x 8" Chunky canvas
- One 8" x 8" Fancy Backed canvas
- Lavender paint
- 2 hinges
- Cardstock
- Transparency
- Ribbon
- Silk daisies
- Chipboard (letters, heart)
- Sleeping Beauty Doll - *The Disney Store*
- English 111 Vouace BT font
- Purse handle and hardware
- Staple gun
- Photo Tape adhesive
- Glossy Accents adhesive

INSTRUCTIONS:

1. Paint outside of both canvases. Let dry. Paint inside of Chunky shadowbox frame. Let dry.
2. Cover both canvases with sheer fabric and fasten the fabric with a staple gun.
3. Mark the canvases for hinges, making sure that the painted sides are on the outside. Hinge the canvases together.
4. Mark holes on the top of the chunky canvas for the purse handle. Attach the handle.
5. **Front cover:** Cut cardstock 5" x 8". Adhere the embellished ribbon to the bottom and top.
6. Sew a Running stitch across the top and bottom of the beaded ribbon. Zigzag stitch Pink satin ribbon in place. See photo.
7. Adhere Pink chipboard letters to the center of the cardstock. Adhere flowers in place.
8. To create a closure, adhere the sheer ribbon around both canvases and leave enough on the ends to tie in a bow.
9. Adhere embellished piece of cardstock to Fancy Backed 8" canvas.
10. **Inside left:** Cut cardstock 8" x 8".
11. Print text on transparency. Cut to 8" square.
12. Running stitch the transparency to the cardstock.
13. Adhere cardstock in place.
14. **Inside right:** Cover inside of Chunky canvas with fabric.
15. Cut cardstock 8" x 8". Cut a frame 1½" wide with a 5" square hole in the center.
16. Zigzag stitch around frame, adhere to shadowbox.
17. Adhere the photo.
18. Punch 2 holes side by side in chipboard heart, tie ribbon to the holes. Adhere in place.
19. Cut the "Disneyland 2004" and "Sleeping Beauty's Castle" transparency words to fit. Adhere to canvas with Glossy Accents. Adhere ribbon.
20. Adhere the Sleeping Beauty doll with Glossy Accents. Let the glue dry at least 24 hours.

Booklets with Pages

Hinges make a secure attachment for three, four or more canvas panels. Use a screwdriver to secure hinges with small screws... pieces can sit on a table or hang on the wall.

1. Ink all edges of the canvas.

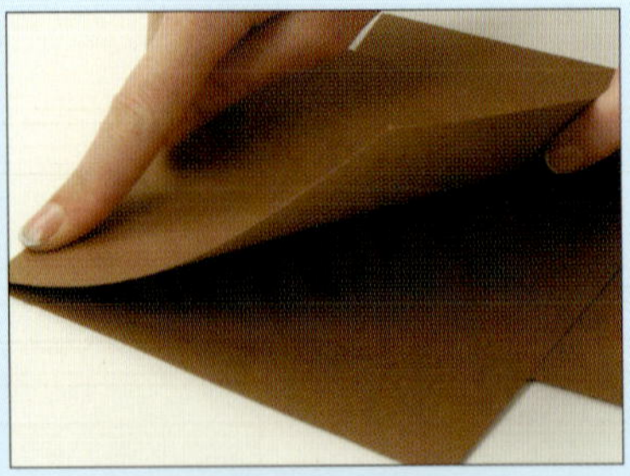

2. Fold 3 pieces of 6" x 12" cardstock in half.

3. Glue cardstock together to form booklet.

4. Staple a piece of ribbon to inside front & back of canvas.

5. Adhere booklet to insides of canvas.

6. Close book and bind with binding tape or cardstock.

7. Ink the binding.

8. Adhere paper to covers to hide binding tape.

9. Embellish booklet.

Vacation

by Emelyn Magpoc

Travel provides a unique opportunity for us to reconnect as a family. We get to spend time together and pay more attention to what matters most in our lives.

Capture the experience in photos that will jog your memory and reignite the emotions that make family vacations so wonderful. This canvas book is an excellent example of easy ways to embellish your pages so you get layouts that are so exciting you can't wait to see what's on the next page.

MATERIALS:
- Two 6" x 6" canvases
- Brown Chalk ink
- Book binding tape
- Cardstock
- Decorative paper - *K&Company*
- Stickers, Metal charms
- Brads, Ribbons, Flowers
- Staple gun
- Glossy Accents adhesive

INSTRUCTIONS:

1. Ink the front, back, and side edges of canvases.

Create the book:

2. Fold 3 pieces of 6" x 12" cardstock in half.
3. Adhere 2 sides together, creating a booklet.
4. Decorate the pages as desired.

Assemble:

5. Adhere the front page of the book inside the front canvas, and the last page to the back canvas.
6. Adhere book binding tape to spine of canvas book.
7. Ink book binding tape.
8. Staple a strip of ribbon to the front and back canvas to make a tie closure.
9. Decorate the front canvas and adhere a piece of decorative paper to the back canvas.

Extreme Rock

by Emelyn Magpoc

Scrapbook your extreme adventures in an exciting canvas book format and relive the adrenaline rush with every page.

Binding tape creates a sturdy but simple hinge that holds this book together.

Attach two layers of silk flower petals to the page with a brad in the center.

MATERIALS:

- Two 4" x 4" canvases
- Chalk ink (Green, Brown)
- Cardstock
- Decorative paper
- Stickers
- Metal charms
- Brads
- Book binding tape
- Silk flowers
- Fabric strips
- Glossy Accents adhesive

INSTRUCTIONS:

1. Ink canvases with Green and then Brown ink.

Create the book:

2. Fold three 4" x 8" cardstock in half.
3. Adhere 2 sides together, creating a booklet.
4. Decorate pages as desired.

Assembly:

5. Adhere the first page to the inside of the front canvas, and the last page to the back canvas.
6. Adhere book binding tape to spine of canvas book.
7. Ink book binding tape.
8. Decorate the front canvas and adhere a piece of decorative paper to the back canvas.

'A' Booklet

by Michelle Tornay

A is for Angel, and this is a book just about her. The journaling inside says, "A daughter is one of the most beautiful gifts this world has to give."

Begin your accordion canvas book with the initial of someone special and write your message of love inside. Add photos and pockets with journaling tags. Someone will be very glad you did.

MATERIALS:
- Two 4" x 4" canvases
- Green paint
- Binding Tape
- Cardstock
- Decorative paper - *Paper Salon*
- Fabric strips
- Chipboard letters
- Chipboard flowers
- Tags
- Zipper pulls
- Ribbon
- Circle embellishment
- Photo Tape adhesive
- Glossy Accents adhesive

INSTRUCTIONS:
1. Paint the canvases. Let dry.
2. Cut 3 paper strips 4" x 12". Score every 4", scoring each strip 3 times.
3. Attach the ends and fold an accordion.
4. Glue the accordion pages together to form a 4 page book. The first and last pages should be left alone.
5. Bind the edge of the book with binding tape.
6. Adhere the first page of the book to a 4" canvas and the last page to the other 4" canvas.
7. Bind the edges of the 2 canvases together with binding tape.
8. Cut two 4" squares of decorative paper. Zigzag stitch around edges.
9. Use a stencil to cut out the letter on front cover paper.
10. Mount papers to the outside of the book.
11. Adhere ribbon, flower, and zipper pulls to the front of the book.
12. Decorate the inside of the canvas with quotes, paper pockets, photos, and tags.

Being a Girl

by Suzy West

The journaling really makes this book special. The foldout page lists Angel's favorite food, shirt, store, performer, song, book, and jewelry. The last page is titled "Before I die I want to..." and provides a touching picture of the dreams this young woman has.

MATERIALS:
- Two 4" x 8" canvases
- Green paint
- Ink pads
- Binding Tape
- Cardstock
- Decorative paper - *MOD*
- Ribbon, Fabric
- Rub-Ons, Tags
- Photo Tape adhesive
- Black marker
- Glossy Accents adhesive

INSTRUCTIONS:

1. Paint canvases. Let dry.
2. Place one canvas on top of the other as though they are the covers of a book. Cut 6 binding strips 1½" x 5". Adhere binding strips to form a hinge, overlapping strips as needed.

Front of the book: Cut and glue cardstock to front canvas. Cut decorative paper with a scallop edge. Adhere straight edges to the book, leaving scallop free of glue to form a pocket. Add fabric strips to the tags and tuck them under the scallop. Create a title.

Inside of the book: Create pages before gluing the book to canvases. Cut cardstock the height of canvas. Crease and fold in accordion style. The longer you want your book, the more paper you use. Adhere all the strips together. Fold them like you were flipping pages in a book. Glue the pages together.

Embellish pages: Mat photos on cardstock, adhere as desired. Decorate pages.

Finish: Glue one end of a ribbon to each canvas so the ends will be sandwiched beneath the endpages. Glue the endpages to the canvas. Let the glue dry. Tie the book closed.

Family

by Krista Fernandez

A family is a little world created by love. Your family memories are your most treasured heirlooms. Celebrate them with this fun canvas book decorated in lively colors and stuffed with happy thoughts.

Looking for a fun idea for page turners? Check out this fresh idea - metal rimmed tags attached with split rings! Black cardstock pages trimmed in a scallop edge provide the perfect place to attach interesting tags.

MATERIALS:
- Two 6" x 6" canvases
- Light Pink acrylic paint
- Binding Tape
- Black cardstock
- Decorative paper - *SEI*
- Rub-On letters, stickers - *SEI*
- Button, Flower charm, Flower brad
- Tags, Ribbon, Flowers
- Heart punch, Circle punch
- Scalloped scissors, Staples, Pins
- Fonts: Constitution, Extra - *Creating Keepsakes*
- Photo Tape adhesive
- Glossy Accents adhesive

Computer print words and add stickers. Pin a ribbon to one page, and add a small silk flower. Secure large black rickrack and a metal rim tag to the edges.

INSTRUCTIONS:
1. Paint all canvas surfaces. Let dry.
2. Cut 3 strips of Black cardstock $5\frac{7}{8}$" x $11\frac{3}{4}$". Fold all in half.
3. Stack cardstock together and bind with binding tape.
4. Cut the ends of the cardstock with decorative scissors.
5. Embellish the book with photos, ribbon, flowers, tags and other accents.
6. Adhere the book to the back sides of the canvas.
7. Bind the entire canvas book with binding tape.
8. Paint the binding tape to match the book.
9. Embellish the cover.

Simple Canvas Displays

Display precious photos and memories every day. You'll love these attractive canvas panels with photos of loved ones, sentimental titles, embellishments and special events.

Simple canvases can be displayed on your favorite table or right on the wall.

1. Paint the canvas.

2. Embellish canvases as desired.

3. Mount canvas on an easel or hang canvas on the wall.

Follow Your Dreams

by Suzy West

Why put a lovely photo in an ordinary frame?

Make it extra special and display it as embellished canvas art on a table easel. This stand-alone 8" canvas is the perfect size to show off your favorite 5 by 7 photography.

MATERIALS:
- One 8" x 8" canvas
- Ink
- Cardstock
- Decorative paper
- Rub-On, Metal corner
- White daisy trim
- Silk daisy
- Foam brush
- Circle punch
- Photo Tape adhesive
- Glossy Accents adhesive

INSTRUCTIONS:
1. Pour ink onto foam brush and paint all over canvas. Let dry.
2. Adhere cardstock, paper and photo to the canvas.
3. Adhere metal corner with Glossy Accents.
4. Punch out paper circle and adhere in place.
5. Adhere flower with Glossy Accents.
6. Add ribbon and title rub-on.
7. Ink around the canvas edges.

Baby

by Emelyn Magpoc

It's baby's first Easter! Surround that special photo with soft spring colors that look great in a baby's room.

MATERIALS:
- One 8" x 8" canvas
- Pink paint
- Moss Chalk ink
- Decorative paper - *Chatterbox*
- Fabric strips
- Wood letter
- Sandpaper
- Photo Tape adhesive
- Glossy Accents adhesive

INSTRUCTIONS:
1. Paint canvas and wood letter. Let dry. Lightly sand the wood letter.
2. Tie fabric strip to the letter.
3. Tie fabric strips to a ⅞" wide strip of decorative paper.
4. Ink the edges of the background paper and adhere to canvas.
5. Tear a paper mat for the photo.
6. Adhere mat, photo, wood letter and paper strip in place.

Grace

by Krista Fernandez

Grace is a vibrant, happy little girl with a smile that melts hearts. Complement this great photo with a collage background that matches the print in her dress.

MATERIALS:
- One 8" x 8" canvas
- Moss e-z walnut tintz - *Fiber Scraps*
- Cardstock
- Decorative paper - *Kopp Designs*
- Rickrack, Ribbon
- Embroidery floss
- Chipboard letter
- Buttons
- Silk flowers
- 2¾" circle punch
- Photo Tape adhesive
- Glossy Accents adhesive

INSTRUCTIONS:
1. Cover canvas with papers and cardstock.
2. Adhere photo to the canvas and line the seams of the decorative papers with rickrack.
3. Tint the monogram with walnut ink. Coat with Glossy Accents. Let dry.
4. Punch a paper circle. Zigzag stich around the edge. Thread ribbon ends through sides of the circle and knot. Adhere circle to canvas, wrap ribbon ends around to back. Staple ribbons to the back of the canvas.
5. Tie floss through buttons. Adhere flowers and buttons.

Krista

by Krista Fernandez

The butterflies resting on Krista's shoulder are just as beautiful as her photograph. This gorgeous piece of summer art will brighten up any space in your home.

INSTRUCTIONS:

1. Ink the edges of decorative paper and adhere to canvas.
2. Dry emboss swirls into a square piece of metal. Cut in half diagonally and adhere to the corners of the canvas.
3. With your finger, lightly rub on metallic coloring on the metal corners.
4. Adhere photo.
5. Embellish tags and adhere to canvas.
6. Adhere butterflies.

MATERIALS:

- One 12" x 12" canvas
- Van Dyke Brown ink
- Decorative paper
- Tags
- Ribbon
- Butterflies
- Metallic accents, Metal sheet
- Embossing stencil and stylus
- Pure Imagination font - 2peasinabucket.com
- Photo Tape adhesive

MATERIALS:

- One 14" x 14" Natural canvas
- Van Dyke Brown ink
- Decorative paper
- Letter stickers
- Ribbon
- Twine
- Diecut tag and sticker
- Metal word dots
- Wood letter tag
- Photo Tape adhesive
- Diamond Glaze
- Pop Up Glue Dots

INSTRUCTIONS:

1. Ink the edges of the canvas.
2. Cut and tear papers as desired. Ink edges. Adhere papers to canvas.
3. Adhere photo.
4. Adhere ribbons along edge of photo with Diamond Glaze.
5. Adhere metal word dot with glue dots.
6. For title, ink wooden tags and tie with twine onto ribbon.
7. Adhere ribbon to decorative paper.
8. Adhere wooden tags in each stripe with Diamond Glaze.
9. Adhere stickers and tag in place.

Our Lil' Stinker

by Emelyn Magpoc

Whether the kids are decked out in their favorite Halloween costume or merely in their new Superman pajamas, your whole family will enjoy viewing their story on canvas.

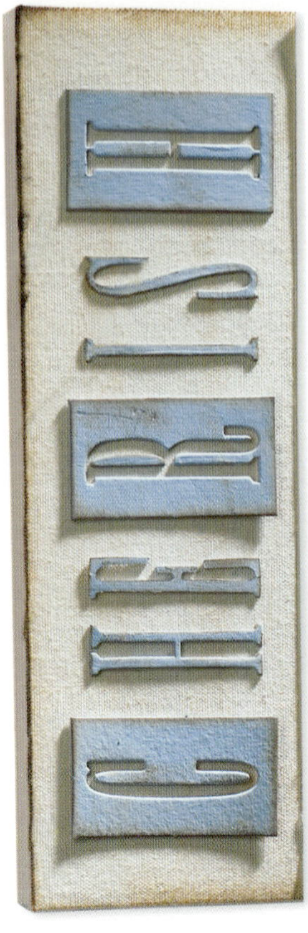

Cherish

by Michelle Tornay

Soft shades of beautiful blues blend together in a canvas your family will truly cherish.

MATERIALS:
- One 12" x 12" Natural canvas
- Paint (White, Light Blue)
- Van Dyke Brown ink
- Decorative paper - *K&Company*
- 2 wood frames
- Blue silk flowers
- Metal button
- Chipboard letters
- Ribbon
- Photo Tape adhesive

INSTRUCTIONS:
1. Paint the frames and chipboard letters. Let dry.
2. Ink the edges of the canvas, frames, and chipboard letters.
3. Cut patterned paper 9" x 12", 4" x 6", and 1" x 9'. Ink all paper edges. Sew a Zigzag stitch around the edges of the papers.
4. Adhere chipboard letters to canvas.
5. Tie the ribbon around the frame.
6. Adhere papers to the canvas as in photo.
7. Adhere the flower and metal button to the 1" strip of paper.
8. Adhere photo and frame to the canvas.

INSTRUCTIONS:

1. Paint large canvas with 2 coats. Let dry.
2. Ink the edges of the striped decorative paper with Brown. Adhere to canvas.
3. Adhere ribbon along edge of Brown paper. Tie small ribbon bows. Adhere in place.
4. Adhere sheer ribbon on top border.
5. Ink 6" canvas edges with Pink. Ink paper edges with Brown.
6. Adhere papers and photos to 6" canvases.
7. Staple the 6" canvases to the large canvas from the back.
8. Create title using rub-on, chipboard letters, and flower.
9. Adhere flower bouquet in place.

Girls

by Emelyn Magpoc

This bouquet of flowers adds a sweet final touch to an already pretty scene. Add a bit of feminine sparkle to your home with this delightful canvas art.

MATERIALS:

- One 12" x 24" canvas
- Two 6" x 6" Natural canvases
- Pink paint
- Ink (Brown, Pink)
- Decorative paper
- Chipboard letters
- Letter stickers
- Rub-On
- Ribbon
- Flowers
- Staple gun
- Diamond Glaze adhesive
- Photo Tape adhesive

MATERIALS:
- One 12" x 12" canvas
- Pink paint
- Van Dyke Brown ink
- Decorative paper - *Foofala*
- Ribbon
- Chipboard heart
- Heart shaped charm
- Rubber stamps - *Technique Tuesday*
- Hole punch
- Photo Tape adhesive
- Glossy Accents adhesive

Puppy Love

by Michelle Tornay

Love describes this subject perfectly. The stamped title, layering and small accents create a setting that draws attention to this touching photo.

INSTRUCTIONS:
1. Paint the edges of the canvas. Let dry.
2. Ink the edges of the 12" x 12" paper.
3. Cut patterned paper 10" x 11". Ink the edges. Adhere to the background paper.
4. Zigzag stitch around edge of the 10" x 11" paper.
5. Punch 2 holes in the upper left hand side of the photo. Tie ribbons and charm to the photo
6. Adhere photo in place.
7. Punch 2 holes in the middle of the chipboard heart. Add a ribbon bow.
8. Stamp letters and adhere the chipboard heart.
9. Adhere to the canvas.